Snow Ponies

Snow Ponies

By CYNTHIA COTTEN

Illustrated by JASON COCKCROFT

HENRY HOLT AND COMPANY ❧ NEW YORK

Henry Holt and Company, LLC
Publishers since 1866
115 West 18th Street
New York, New York 10011
Henry Holt is a registered trademark
of Henry Holt and Company, LLC

Published in Canada by Fitzhenry & Whiteside Ltd.,
195 Allstate Parkway, Markham, Ontario L3R 4T8.

Library of Congress Cataloging-in-Publication Data
Cotten, Cynthia.
Snow ponies / Cynthia Cotten; illustrated by Jason Cockcroft.
Summary: When Old Man Winter lets his snow
ponies out of the barn, they run into the world,
and everything that they touch turns white.
[1. Winter—Fiction. 2. Snow—Fiction. 3. Ponies—Fiction.]
I. Cockcroft, Jason, ill. II. Title.
PZ7.C82865Sn 2001 [E]—dc21 00-40986

ISBN 0-8050-6063-4
First Edition—2001
Printed in the United States of America
on acid-free paper. ∞
1 3 5 7 9 10 8 6 4 2

The artist used acrylic paint on paper
to create the illustrations for this book.

On a cold, gray day, Old Man Winter walks out to his barn and opens the door.

"Hello, my pretty ones," he says. "It's a fine day for a romp." The snow ponies toss their heads and paw the floor.

One by one, he opens the stall doors and takes the snow ponies to a pen beside the barn. Soon the pen is full of ponies, jostling and prancing. Their breath makes white clouds that rise above their heads.

When all the ponies are in the pen, Old Man Winter walks among them, patting backs and rubbing noses.

"Are you ready?" he asks.

The ponies stamp their feet and shake their heads in reply.

Unfastening the gate, Old Man Winter
claps his hands. "Go on!" he calls.
And he leans against the fence and laughs
with delight.

The snow ponies flow out of the pen into the wide openness beyond the gate. Faster and faster they go, manes flying, tails streaming out behind them. Their feet make no sound on the cold, hard ground, and whatever they touch turns white.

The ponies are playful and full of energy. In a
flurry, they canter and call to each other. Their
whinnies and whickers whistle through the trees.

Little by little, they grow faster, louder. Creatures
of forest and field shiver and get out of their way.
The white-tailed deer waits in a woody thicket.

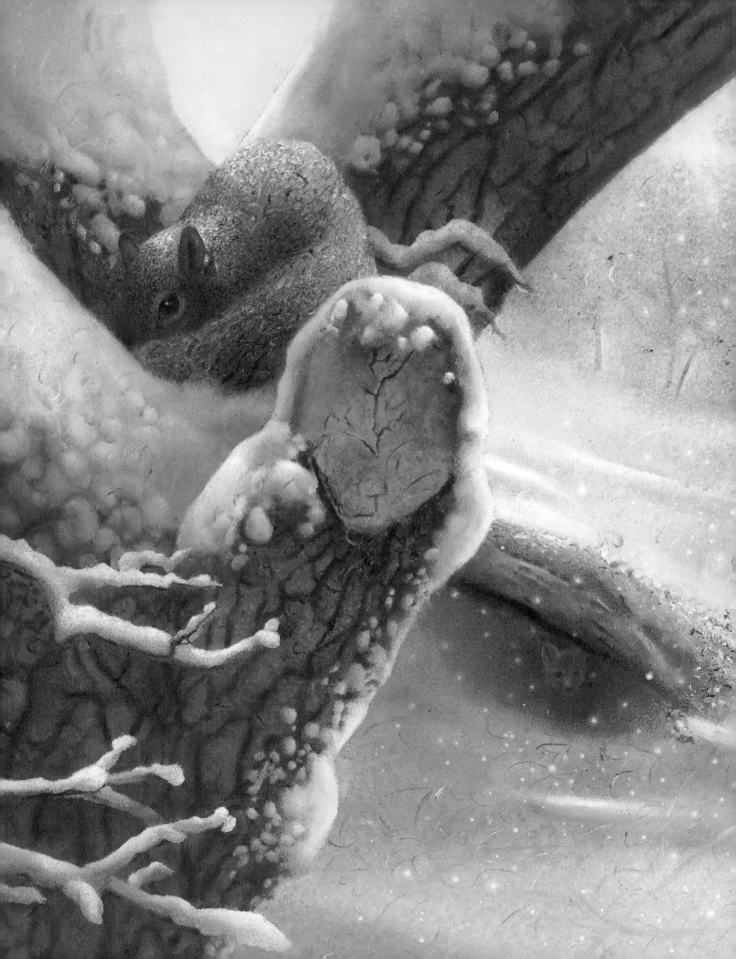

The gray squirrel curls up in the bare-branched oak.
The red fox snuggles in his cozy den.

And the songbirds hide in the holly bush.
They watch and listen as the snow ponies frolic.

The ponies buck and rear and race. They spin and kick up their heels. Little clouds of snow whirl around them. Flakes fly off branches as they snort and blow. Wilder and wilder their play becomes. Through the woods and across the fields they gallop. They leap over fences and nip at each other's heels.

At last the snow ponies begin to tire. Back to the
barn they drift, huddling together. Old Man Winter
opens the door.

"Come, my pretty ones," he says. "Come and rest."

Back in their stalls the snow ponies shake their heads, shuffle their feet, and sigh long sleepy sighs. Old Man Winter rubs them down, covers them with blankets, and quietly shuts the door as he leaves.

The snow ponies close their eyes and slowly, slowly nod off to sleep.

Everything is white, as far as the eye can see.

And Old Man Winter smiles.